Super Science Crosswords

15 Reproducible Crossword Puzzles Using Engaging Diagrams That Help Kids Learn About Plants, Animals, and Other Science Topics You Teach

by Katherine Burkett

SCHOLASTIC
PROFESSIONAL BOOKS

New York • Toronto • London • Auckland • Sydney • Mexico City • New Dehli • Hong Kong

In loving memory of Damien Kong, whose love and knowledge of animals live on in the programs of the Miami Metrozoo, and within these pages.

Special thanks to

Caroline Conway of The Living Desert
Raoul Lopez of the National Severe Storm Laboratory
Andrew Modest, MD, of Harvard Medical School
John Rojie of The Pennsylvania State University
David Rothstein of the University of Michigan
Paul Sieswerda of the New York Aquarium
Frank Summers of The American Museum of Natural History

COVER AND INTERIOR DESIGN BY
Holly Grundon

ILLUSTRATIONS BY
Patricia Wynne & Dianne Gaspas-Ettl

ISBN # 0-590-64457-2

Table of Contents

How To Use This Book

The crossword puzzles in this book are designed to help your students learn important science content in a fun way. They're a great way to address many of the content standards promoted by the National Science Education Standards (see below). They're also excellent practice in "reading for information," an invaluable skill that students can use throughout the curriculum. As a bonus, they're easy to use, providing instant science activities. Used at the beginning of a unit, they're an excellent introduction to a new science topic. They can also serve as an important review at the end of a unit.

Each activity includes:

- detailed diagrams that teach students about the topic
- a crossword puzzle
- a crossword answer key
- background information and extension activities

What to Do:

Photocopy the diagram pages for each student or group of students. For the double pages, cut or fold along the dashed lines. Align the pages, then tape them together. Distribute the diagrams along with their respective crossword puzzles. You may want to encourage students to do research and color in the diagrams correctly for extra credit.

National Science Education Standards

The activities in this book support these content standards:

Grades K-4
- Characteristics of organisms
- Life cycles of organisms
- Organisms and environments
- Personal health

Grades 5-8
- Structure and function in living systems
- Populations and ecosystems
- Diversity and adaptations of organisms
- Earth in the solar system
- Personal health

Boning Up on Your Skeleton

Your bones protect your organs and hold you up. Together with your muscles, your bones also help you move around.

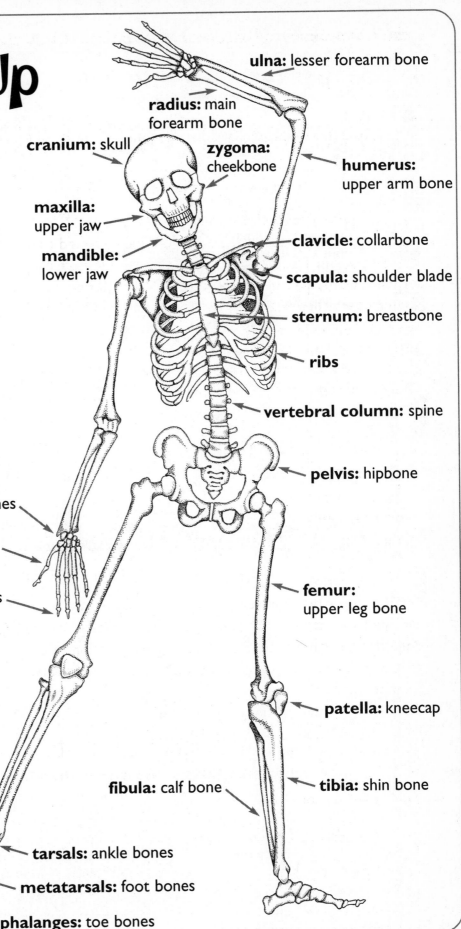

ulna: lesser forearm bone

radius: main forearm bone

cranium: skull

zygoma: cheekbone

humerus: upper arm bone

maxilla: upper jaw

mandible: lower jaw

clavicle: collarbone

scapula: shoulder blade

sternum: breastbone

ribs

vertebral column: spine

pelvis: hipbone

carpals: wrist bones

metacarpals: hand bones

phalanges: finger bones

femur: upper leg bone

patella: kneecap

tibia: shin bone

fibula: calf bone

tarsals: ankle bones

metatarsals: foot bones

phalanges: toe bones

Did You Know?

Kids are "bonier" than grown-ups. You were born with more than 300 bones. As you grow, some of those bones fuse together. By the time you're finished growing, you'll have only 206 bones left!

Background Info

Your skeleton has three main jobs: to support your body, help you move, and protect vital internal organs. Bones are designed to be strong, but light. They're made up of tough minerals like calcium and phosphorus, and have air pockets inside that help cut down on their weight. Many bones have a tube-like shape, which helps them stand up under heavier loads.

The bone marrow inside your bones also has an important job—producing red blood cells, white blood cells, and platelets.

Taking It Further

Bones give an animal its shape. Display illustrations of animal skeletons and invite students to guess which animals the skeletons belong to. As an extension, have students compare an animal skeleton to the human-skeleton diagram. Ask them to look for bones in common, such as cranium, mandible, vertebral column, pelvis, etc.

Joints allow our skeleton to move. What would life be like without them? Have students tape popsicle sticks to the front and back of their index finger. (They can also try using rulers secured with strips of cloth for larger joints.) What tasks (e.g., writing or turning the page of a book) are difficult to do without those joints?

What happens when bones break? Invite a health-care professional to speak to your class about mending broken bones. They may be able to bring in X-rays of broken bones or healing bones held together with pins or screws.

Crossword Answers

Boning Up on Your Skeleton

Across

5. The bone between the inside of your elbow and your wrist is your _____.

8. This bone protects your brain.

9. Your upper leg bone is attached to your torso at your _____.

11. The bone between your hip and knee is your _____.

15. Sit up straight. You just used your spine, or _____.

19. Your upper teeth are rooted in your _____.

20. Your lesser forearm bone is called your _____.

21. This bone runs parallel to 12 Down.

22. Your foot bones are called _____.

Down

1. The bones between your metatarsals and your tibia are called _____.

2. Your _____ protect your heart and lungs.

3. To open your mouth, you need to move your _____.

4. Some muscles that help you grin are attached to each cheekbone, or _____.

6. Your upper ribs connect in front to a bone called the _____.

7. Your toes and fingers are all called _____.

10. The bones in the palm of your hand are called _____.

12. Your calf bone is called your _____.

13. The round, flat bone that protects the joint between your upper and lower leg bones is called your _____.

14. The _____ connects your shoulder to your forearm.

16. Your wrist bones are called _____.

17. Both your _____ stretch from shoulder to shoulder in front.

18. A shoulder blade is called a _____.

Gut Feelings

Food gives you energy to walk, talk, think, and more. How does food turn into energy your body can use? Follow a hamburger on a fantastic voyage through your body.

1. Sharp front teeth, called **incisors**, tear off a chunk of burger.

2. **Salivary glands** start pumping, moistening food to make it easier to swallow. Saliva also contains *enzymes*, proteins that begin breaking down the chemicals in food.

3. The **tongue** guides the burger piece to the back teeth, called **molars**. The wide and flat molars are perfect for grinding the meat and bread to pulpy mush. The tongue then pushes the mush to the back of the mouth. Gulp!

4. the **esophagus**, just like a hand squeezes toothpaste out of a tube. This squeezing is called *peristalsis*. Peristalsis pushes the mashed-up burger to the stomach in about seven seconds—even if you're standing on your head.

Muscles squeeze food down

esophagus

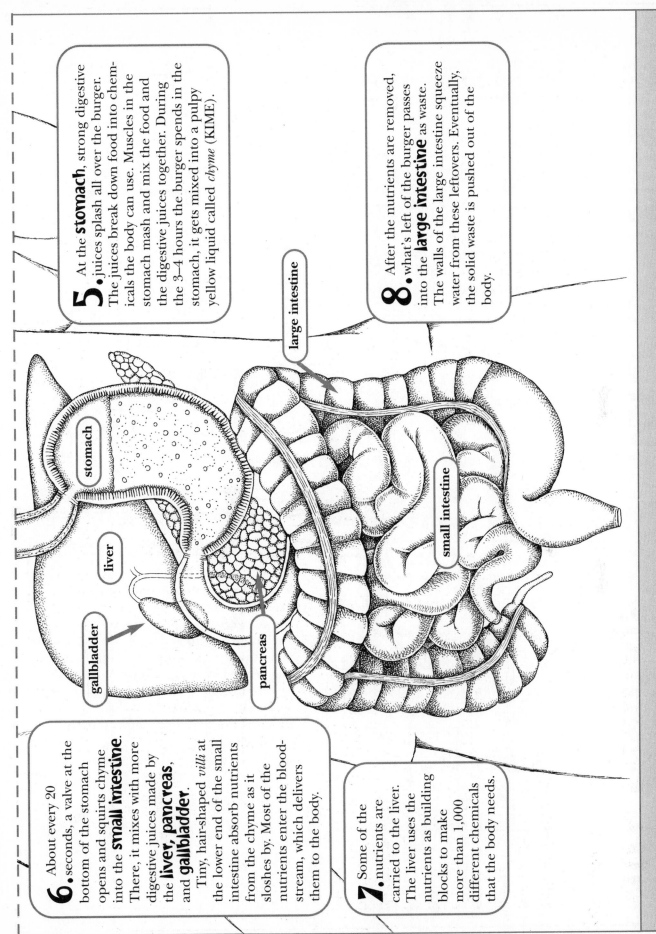

5. At the **stomach**, strong digestive juices splash all over the burger. The juices break down food into chemicals the body can use. Muscles in the stomach mash and mix the food and the digestive juices together. During the 3–4 hours the burger spends in the stomach, it gets mixed into a pulpy yellow liquid called *chyme* (KIME).

6. About every 20 seconds, a valve at the bottom of the stomach opens and squirts chyme into the **small intestine.** There, it mixes with more digestive juices made by the **liver, pancreas, and gallbladder.**

Tiny, hair-shaped *villi* at the lower end of the small intestine absorb nutrients from the chyme as it sloshes by. Most of the nutrients enter the bloodstream, which delivers them to the body.

7. Some of the nutrients are carried to the liver. The liver uses the nutrients as building blocks to make more than 1,000 different chemicals that the body needs.

8. After the nutrients are removed, what's left of the burger passes into the **large intestine** as waste. The walls of the large intestine squeeze water from these leftovers. Eventually, the solid waste is pushed out of the body.

stomach

liver

gallbladder

pancreas

large intestine

small intestine

Did You Know? Your digestive tract is more than 20 feet long. Food usually makes the trip in about a day.

Background Info

The digestive system extracts nutrients from food. It does this by physically and chemically breaking food down to the molecular level, absorbing any useful substances, and expelling the waste.

Students will naturally be familiar with the basics of digestion, but may be fuzzy on the details. For instance, the stomach isn't under the navel. Instead, it's above the navel and to the left. The familiar "stomach rumbling" noises are actually made by the small intestine as peristalsis squeezes and squirts food along.

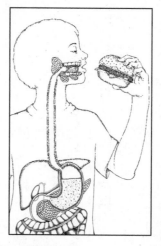

Taking It Further

Have students predict how far food has to travel through their bodies. You can graph predictions on a chalk board, or have students use masking tape to mark the actual lengths along a hall or wall. Then, choose some volunteers to measure out 21 ft. 7 in. of adding machine-tape. Have them divide the tape into these lengths:

- mouth—3 in.
- esophagus—10 in.
- stomach—6 in.
- small intestine—16 ft.
- large intestine—4 ft.

Pass out a crunchy snack (like apple slices or carrots) and some cold water for a little digestive-system investigation. Have students think about eating the snack. Can they feel their mouths "watering"? (If not, have them think about eating their favorite foods instead.) That's the salivary glands in action. Next, have students bite into and chew their foods. Have them notice which teeth they use to take a bite (incisors) and which to mash the food (molars). Have them finish the snack with a swallow of cold water. Can they feel the cold water slide down their esophagus?

Crossword Answers

```
        S A L I V A R Y G L A N D S
  E   V   A                       M
I N C I S O R S                   A
  Z   L   G   M   C               L
  Y   L   E S O P H A G U S       L
  M   I   I   L   Y               I
  E       N   A   M               N
  S       T   R   E               T
          E   S                   E
          S       N U T R I E N T S
          T                       T
  L       I                       I
D I G E S T I V E J U I C E S     N
  V       N                       E
  E       E
  R       S T     P     T
    G A L L B L A D D E R
          O       N     E
          M       C     T
          C       R   T O N G U E
          H       E     H
                  A
          P E R I S T A L S I S
```

Gut Feelings

Across

1. _____ moisten food and make it easier to swallow.

6. _____ help bite into food.

9. This tube connects the mouth and stomach.

10. After the body absorbs _____ from food, what's left is considered waste.

12. _____ in the stomach and small intestine break down food into chemicals the body can use.

16. One of the organs that make digestive juices that are used in the small intestine.

17. In addition to tasting, the _____ moves food around the mouth.

18. This "squeezing" motion pushes food through the esophagus and the rest of the digestive tract.

Down

2. In the _____, water is removed from food waste.

3. Nutrients are absorbed from food in the _____, the longest organ in the digestive system.

4. _____ in saliva begin to break down food.

5. Hair-like _____ soak up nutrients.

7. Wide and flat _____ grind food to a pulp.

8. In the stomach, the food is mixed into a yellow liquid called _____.

11. The _____ uses nutrients from food to form more than 1,000 different chemicals.

13. In the _____, food is mashed and mixed with digestive juices.

14. One of the organs that make digestive juices that are used in the small intestine.

15. Biters and mashers are _____.

Go With the Flow

Take a deep breath. You just sent an incredible amount of oxygen on an expedition deep into your body. Follow the steps below to find out where the oxygen goes, and what it does when it gets there.

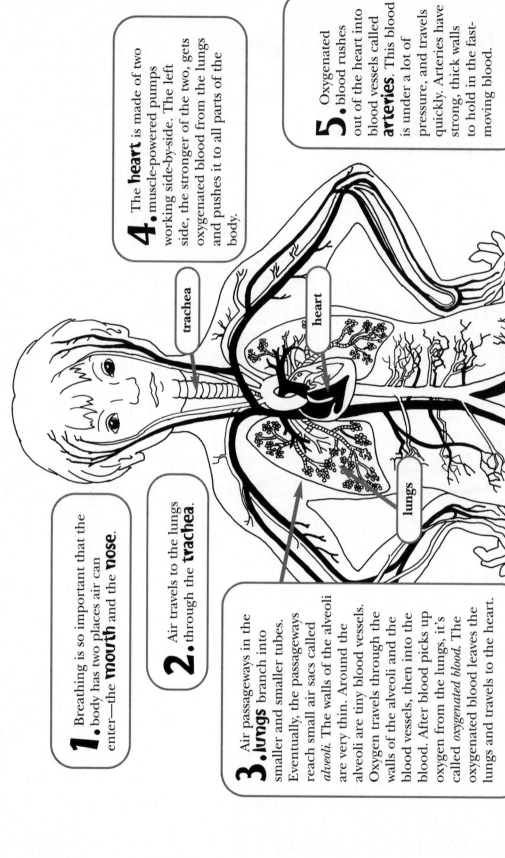

trachea

heart

lungs

1. Breathing is so important that the body has two places air can enter—the **mouth** and the **nose**.

2. Air travels to the lungs through the **trachea.**

3. Air passageways in the **lungs** branch into smaller and smaller tubes. Eventually, the passageways reach small air sacs called *alveoli.* The walls of the alveoli are very thin. Around the alveoli are tiny blood vessels. Oxygen travels through the walls of the alveoli and the blood vessels, then into the blood. After blood picks up oxygen from the lungs, it's called *oxygenated blood.* The oxygenated blood leaves the lungs and travels to the heart.

4. The **heart** is made of two muscle-powered pumps working side-by-side. The left side, the stronger of the two, gets oxygenated blood from the lungs and pushes it to all parts of the body.

5. Oxygenated blood rushes out of the heart into blood vessels called **arteries.** This blood is under a lot of pressure, and travels quickly. Arteries have strong, thick walls to hold in the fast-moving blood.

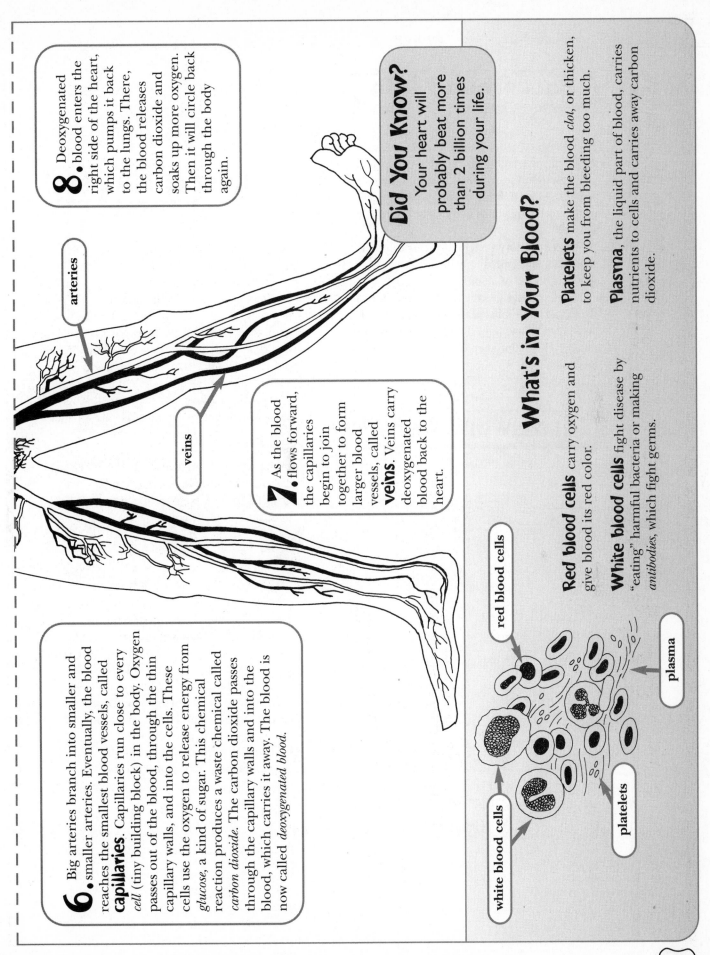

8. Deoxygenated blood enters the right side of the heart, which pumps it back to the lungs. There, the blood releases carbon dioxide and soaks up more oxygen. Then it will circle back through the body again.

arteries

veins

7. As the blood flows forward, the capillaries begin to join together to form larger blood vessels, called **veins**. Veins carry deoxygenated blood back to the heart.

6. Big arteries branch into smaller and smaller arteries. Eventually, the blood reaches the smallest blood vessels, called **capillaries**. Capillaries run close to every *cell* (tiny building block) in the body. Oxygen passes out of the blood, through the thin capillary walls, and into the cells. These cells use the oxygen to release energy from *glucose*, a kind of sugar. This chemical reaction produces a waste chemical called *carbon dioxide*. The carbon dioxide passes through the capillary walls and into the blood, which carries it away. The blood is now called *deoxygenated blood*.

Did You Know?
Your heart will probably beat more than 2 billion times during your life.

What's in Your Blood?

Red blood cells carry oxygen and give blood its red color.

White blood cells fight disease by "eating" harmful bacteria or making *antibodies*, which fight germs.

Platelets make the blood *clot*, or thicken, to keep you from bleeding too much.

Plasma, the liquid part of blood, carries nutrients to cells and carries away carbon dioxide.

red blood cells

white blood cells

platelets

plasma

Background Info

The respiratory system (mouth, nose, trachea, and lungs) and the circulatory system (heart, blood, and blood vessels) work together to bring oxygen to all the cells of the body. They also carry away carbon dioxide.

The circulatory system also carries other important substances to cells, including glucose, a kind of sugar.

Nasal passages warm and humidify the air we inhale. (Air inhaled through the mouth is also warmed and humidified, though not as much.) This helps keep our bodies from losing too much fluid.

Crossword Answers

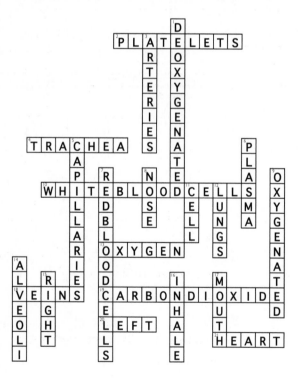

Taking It Further

Red-cabbage juice can help students observe what's in the air they exhale. To make red-cabbage juice, put 2 1/2 cups chopped red cabbage in a pot with 2 cups of water, and heat until boiling. Let the mixture cool, then discard the cabbage and pour the red liquid into a container. Pour 2 tablespoons of red-cabbage juice into a small paper cup for each student. Give each student a drinking straw as well. Have students blow through the straw into the cabbage juice for one minute. What happens to the juice's color? *(The red juice should turn into a lighter color.)* Red-cabbage juice is an acid indicator. When the carbon dioxide students exhale mixes with water, it forms a weak acid and turns the juice into a lighter color.

To help students visualize what's in blood, help them create a model of blood. First, put aside a glass jar of water with a few drops of yellow food coloring mixed in—this is the "plasma," the liquid part of blood. Next, have students use hole punchers to punch out 1,000 "red blood cells" from red plastic covers and 50 "platelets" from brown construction paper. Cut out 2 "white blood cells" from a white plastic grocery bag—they should be several times larger than the red blood cells. Put all the "cells" in a second glass jar. Ask students: How do all these solid blood cells get around the body? *(A liquid is needed.)* Add the "plasma" into the jar. Now, you've got blood!

Go With the Flow

Across

2. _____ in blood keep you from bleeding too much.

4. The air passage between the nose and the lungs

10. These cells fight disease

13. An important gas the body needs

18. These blood vessels carry deoxygenated blood to the heart.

19. Cells produce this waste chemical.

20. The _____ side of the heart pushes oxygenated blood to all parts of the body.

21. Two muscle-powered pumps that work side by side

Down

1. After blood releases oxygen to the cells of the body, the blood becomes _____.

3. These thick-walled blood vessels carry oxygenated blood to the cells in your body.

5. The smallest blood vessels

6. The liquid part of the blood

7. These carry oxygen and give your blood its color.

8. Most people breathe through this.

9. _____ blood travels from the lungs to the heart.

11. Capillaries run close to every _____ in the body.

12. In the _____, oxygen enters the blood and carbon dioxide leaves it.

14. Small air sacs in your lungs

15. The _____ side of the heart pushes deoxygenated blood to your lungs.

16. Breathe in

17. If your nose is stuffed up, you can still breathe through your _____.

The Secret Life of Plants

Plants don't seen very active, but they get a lot done. They gather energy from the sun. They use the energy to grow and make new plants. Read on to find out how.

How Flowers Make Seeds

2. **Stamens** make *pollen*, a powder that flowers need to make seeds. The **anther** is the tip of a stamen. When an insect brushes against an anther, tiny pollen grains stick to its body. The insect carries the pollen to other flowers.

3. A **pistil** has a sticky tip called a **stigma**. When pollen-carrying insects brush up against the stigma, pollen grains stick to it.

1. Colorful **petals** attract insects, like bees and butterflies.

4. A pollen grain grows a tube that travels down through the pistil into the **ovary**.

5. The pollen tube connects to an **ovule**, which contains a tiny plant egg. Part of the pollen travels down the tube and joins with the egg. Once this happens, the egg can grow into a seed.

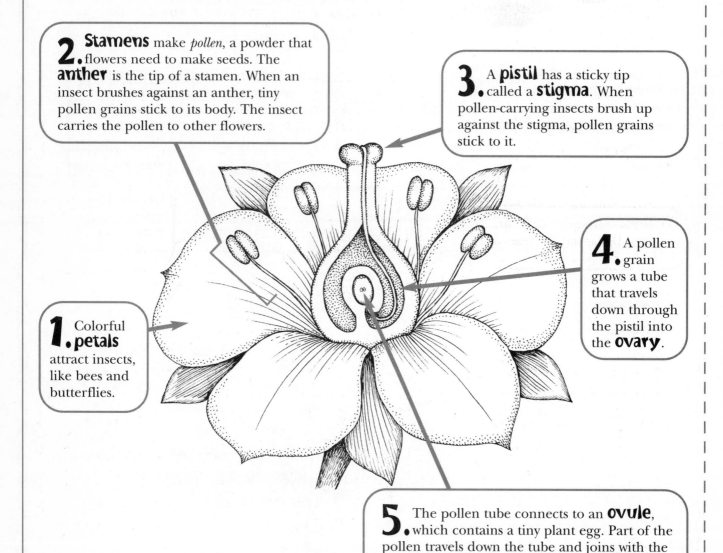

Inside a Seed

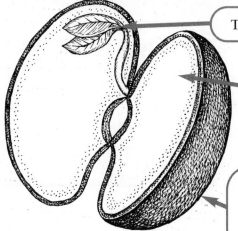

The **embryo** is the tiny plant, ready to grow.

The **cotyledons** hold food stored for the embryo to help it sprout into a tiny plant. Once the plant reaches sunlight, it can make its own food.

The **seed coat** keeps the seed from sprouting before growing conditions are right. For instance, the seed coat may not open until the soil is moist.

Other Plant Parts

Flowers make pollen. They also collect pollen made by other flowers and use it to make seeds.

Leaves soak up sunlight and use it to make food for the plant.

Fruits hold the plant's seeds. Colorful and tasty fruits may attract animals that eat the fruits and scatter the seeds.

Stems hold the plant off the ground. They also contain tiny pipes that carry water, minerals, and food to different parts of the plant.

Roots soak up water and minerals from the soil. They also help anchor the plant in the ground.

Background Info

The plant kingdom consists of more than 400,000 species. Not all plants are as simple as we had labeled on page 17. There are all kinds of variations that can be found in the plant kingdom. For example, scientists don't consider a strawberry (or other berries) as fruit. Rather, it's an enlarged receptacle and the so-called "seeds" are the actual fruits.

Most plants are flowering plants. Non-flowering plants reproduce by shedding spores. Flowering plants, on the other hand, reproduce by making seeds. There are two ways plants can become fertilized. *Cross-pollination*, the most common way, occurs when animals carry pollen grains from the flower of one plant to the flower of another plant. Both plants must be of the same species for fertilization to occur. In *self-pollination*, pollen from a flower's anther (the part that bears the pollen) falls onto the stigma (the part that receives the pollen) of the same flower, or to another flower on the same plant.

Crossword Answers

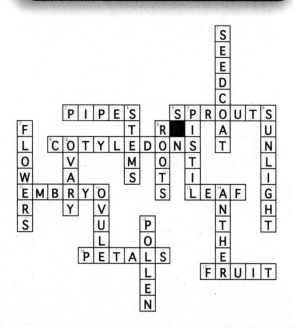

Taking It Further

Ask a local florist to donate tulips or lilies that are past their prime. Pass out one flower per pair of students. (You may also pass out hand lenses, scissors, and round toothpicks to be used as dissection tools.) Using the illustration on page 16, have students identify the different flower parts. To collect pollen for better viewing, have students lightly press a clear piece of tape on the anther, then stick the tape to a piece of paper.

Soak dried lima beans for 2 or 3 days and pass out one bean per student. (Have extras on hand, in case a bean is damaged.) Show students how to remove the seed coat and gently pry the seed open. Then ask them to find the parts labeled in the diagram on page 17.

How tall can a baby plant grow using only the energy stored in its cotyledons? To find out, have your class compare seedlings growing in the dark with those growing in light. Give each group of students two cups of soil and four seeds. Have them plant two seeds per cup, leaving space between them, then water the soil. Keep cups in a dark, cool place until the seeds begin to sprout. Then, move one cup to a windowsill while the other stays in the dark. Students should check the plants daily and measure their growth. The seedlings in the light will grow steadily, sending out leaves to collect energy from sunlight. The seedlings in the dark will grow quickly, depleting the energy stored in their cotyledons while stretching upward in search of sunlight.

The Secret Life of Plants

Across

2. Water, minerals, and food travel through _____ in a plant's stems.

4. A seed uses its stored food when it _____.

9. Without _____, a baby plant wouldn't have the food energy it needs to grow into the sunlight.

11. Before a seed sprouts, the tiny plant inside is called an _____.

13. A piece of spinach is a _____.

16. A flower's scent and colorful _____ attract insects.

17. A tasty _____ attracts hungry animals that can help the plant scatter its seeds.

Down

1. A delicate plant embryo is protected by a _____.

3. _____ hold a plant off the ground.

5. A flower's _____ has a sticky tip called a stigma.

6. A leaf makes food using energy from _____.

7. _____ are a plant's seed factories.

8. _____ soak up water from the soil.

10. Pollen grows a tube that travels down to the flower's _____.

12. Each _____ contains a tiny egg.

14. When an insect brushes against the _____, it picks up some of the flower's pollen.

15. A seed forms when an egg is joined by _____.

Leafy Green Food Factories

Plants make their own food, using a process called *photosynthesis* (foe-toe-SIN-theh-sus). Through photosynthesis, plants take energy from sunlight and change it into food. Follow these steps to find out how.

1. Sunlight shines on the leaves. (Other green parts of the plant may also perform photosynthesis, but leaves do most of the work.)

2. A gas called **carbon dioxide** soaks into little holes in the leaves called *stomata*. Some carbon dioxide comes from animals like you. When you breathe in, your lungs take oxygen from the air. When you breathe out, they release carbon dioxide.

4. Using energy from sunlight, leaves change water and carbon dioxide into plant food and oxygen. This is **photosynthesis** in action.

5. Oxygen is released through the stomata, the same tiny holes that let in carbon dioxide.

3. The plant's roots soak up **water**. The water then travels up through the stems to the leaves.

6. The plant food starts out as a simple sugar called **glucose**. The plant uses any glucose it needs right away. Then it changes the rest into other kinds of food that are easier to store. These are the foods that animals get from eating plants.

Factory Tour

Here's a close-up look at the inside of a leaf.

The **cuticle** is a waxy outer layer. It helps the leaf keep the water it needs.

Layers of cells on the top and bottom of the leaf make up the **epidermis**. Like our skin, the epidermis protects the more tender inside of the leaf.

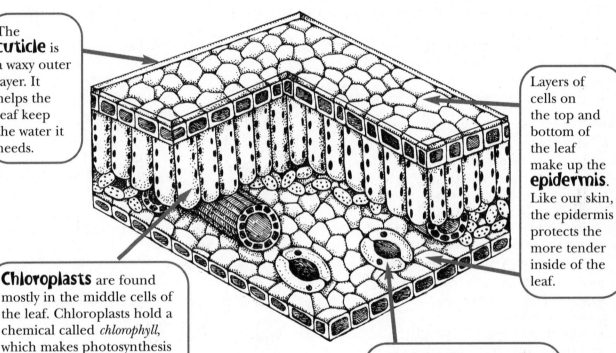

Chloroplasts are found mostly in the middle cells of the leaf. Chloroplasts hold a chemical called *chlorophyll*, which makes photosynthesis possible. Chlorophyll also gives leaves their green color.

The **stomata** let carbon dioxide in and oxygen out.

How Plants Store Food
Plants use glucose to make these different kinds of food.

Sucrose easily travels to different parts of the plant through the stems. Sugar-beet plants store sucrose in their large roots. The roots can be harvested and used to make table sugar.

The plant uses **cellulose** to build the walls of its cells. When you eat lettuce or celery, you get a lot of cellulose.

Starch is stored in the leaves, stems, or roots. Potatoes are underground stems that store a lot of starch.

Plants can also use glucose to make **fats** and **proteins**. Peas, beans, and other seeds are often rich in fats and proteins.

Background Info

Scientists don't completely understand how photosynthesis works. They know it occurs in two stages, each consisting of multiple steps. In the first stage, leaves harvest light energy and store it as chemical energy. The second stage uses the chemical energy to make glucose from water and carbon dioxide, and release oxygen waste into the air.

Every year, plants release about 10 to 100 billion tons of oxygen. Interestingly, plants take oxygen from the air during *respiration*—the process by which plant cells get energy from glucose. However, they use much less oxygen than they produce.

In the fall, some plants lose the chlorophyll from their leaves. That's when leaves "change color." (The mineral components that make up chlorophyll are stored in the plant's stems and used for the next year's leaves.) With the green chlorophyll gone, other pigments in the leaves can shine through.

Taking It Further

Help students trace every part of their lunch back to photosynthesis. Fruits and vegetables will be easy, since they are plant parts. Most common lunch meats come from animals that eat plant parts, including grain. Milk is made by cows, who eat grain. Highly processed foods may be more tricky to track. Chocolate and sugar are both plant products. An encyclopedia can tell kids more. Some ingredients, such as table salt, are inorganic, and therefore don't come from plants. However, they won't be the source of calories in a dish.

Crossword Answers

Leafy Green Food Factories

Across

1. Plant cell walls are made of _____.

4. Your lungs release this gas that plants need for photosynthesis.

5. This waxy outer layer keeps a leaf from drying out.

6. _____ get food and oxygen from plants.

8. During _____, plants make food using energy from the sun.

12. Plants make this gas you breathe.

14. Sucrose, starch, fat, and protein are all kinds of _____ we get from eating plants.

16. When you eat potatoes, you are getting a kind of stored plant food called _____.

Down

2. Like your skin, a leaf's _____ protects its more tender inner cells.

3. _____ carry water from the roots to the leaves.

5. _____ are found mostly in the middle of a leaf.

7. This green chemical makes photosynthesis possible.

8. _____ make their own food using carbon dioxide, water, and energy from sunlight.

9. This form of plant food easily travels to different parts of the plant.

10. These tiny holes let carbon dioxide in and oxygen out.

11. Most leaves are wide and flat. This shape helps make it easier for them to collect energy from _____.

13. Plant food starts out as this simple sugar.

15. Plants' roots soak up this important ingredient for photosynthesis.

Seeds on the Move

Where's the best place for a seed to sprout? Far away from its mother plant. If a plant's seeds fell straight to the ground, the plant and its offspring would have to compete for sunlight, water, and nutrients from the soil. Only a few could survive. So how can a seed find its own place to grow? Read on for some surprising seed-travel tales.

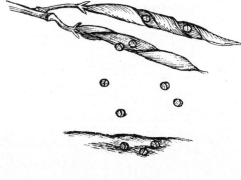

Long-distance Launchers ▲

A **witch-hazel** tree can send its seeds up to 30 feet away. When a seedpod opens, it pinches one end of the smooth seed inside. The seed shoots out of the pod, like soap slipping out of your hand.

Mud Trekkers

Many **wildflower** seeds fall straight to the ground. During rain, they get mixed into the mud. If a passing paw or boot picks up some mud, the seeds go along for the ride. When the mud dries and falls off, the seeds have a new place to sprout. ▼

Fluffy Fliers ▲

This puffy ball is a **dandelion** seed head. Each bit of fluff is like a little parachute with a seed dangling at the bottom. When a breeze blows, the parachutes catch the wind. They break away from the ball and carry the seed to a new patch of ground.

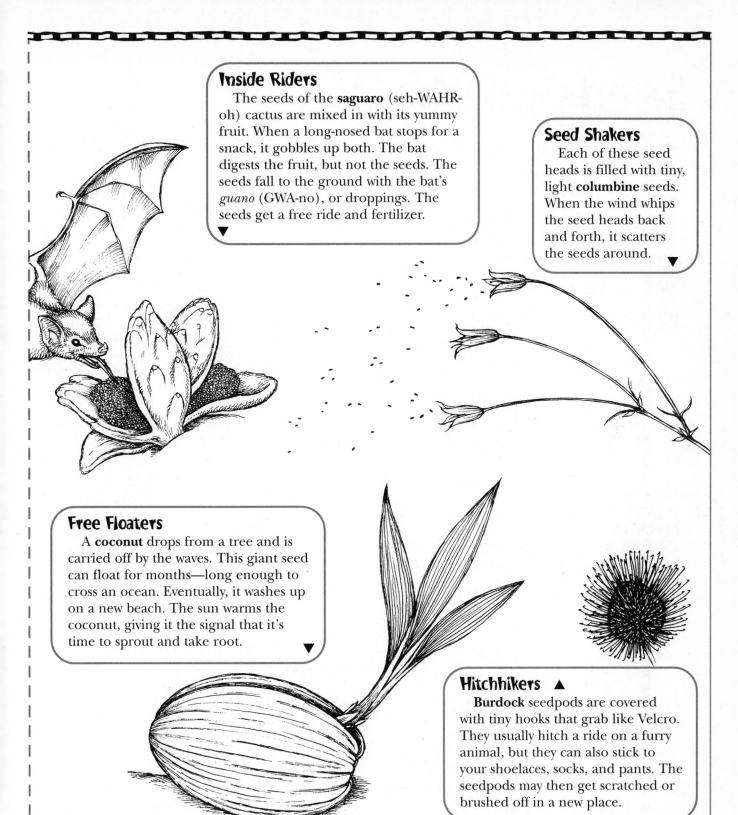

Inside Riders

The seeds of the **saguaro** (seh-WAHR-oh) cactus are mixed in with its yummy fruit. When a long-nosed bat stops for a snack, it gobbles up both. The bat digests the fruit, but not the seeds. The seeds fall to the ground with the bat's *guano* (GWA-no), or droppings. The seeds get a free ride and fertilizer. ▼

Seed Shakers

Each of these seed heads is filled with tiny, light **columbine** seeds. When the wind whips the seed heads back and forth, it scatters the seeds around. ▼

Free Floaters

A **coconut** drops from a tree and is carried off by the waves. This giant seed can float for months—long enough to cross an ocean. Eventually, it washes up on a new beach. The sun warms the coconut, giving it the signal that it's time to sprout and take root. ▼

Hitchhikers ▲

Burdock seedpods are covered with tiny hooks that grab like Velcro. They usually hitch a ride on a furry animal, but they can also stick to your shoelaces, socks, and pants. The seedpods may then get scratched or brushed off in a new place.

Did You Know?

If conditions aren't right, a seed won't sprout. Some seeds can sit for years, waiting for the right temperature and amount of moisture. Lotus seeds have been known to sprout more than 200 years after they were formed!

Background Info

Plants produce far more seeds than can sprout and survive. That's because there's a good chance that many of the seeds won't land where conditions are right for sprouting. Or they may sprout, but not be able to get the sunlight, water, or nutrients they need to survive.

Crossword Answers

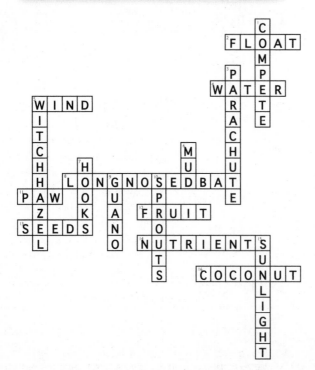

Taking It Further

Pass out dried beans and have students work in pairs to invent ways to disperse these seeds. Provide a variety of materials for kids to work with, including tape, glue, cotton balls, Styrofoam, cloth, bits of Velcro, toothpicks, rubber bands, etc. Students who are designing a floating seed can test it in a small cup of water. Students designing a flying seed can test it with a fan. After the pairs present their seeds to the class, you can tie them to an empty branch for display.

To illustrate how plants produce extra seeds, try this math activity: Give each group of students a sliced apple and several spoons. Students should use the spoons to "dissect" the apple and count the seeds in it. Work with the class to find the average number of seeds in their apples. Then, have students think of an apple tree that grows 800 apples per year. Ask: How many seeds does the tree make altogether? *(Your class average times 800)* Say each seed grew into a tree and each tree grew the same number of seeds as the mother tree. How many seeds would they make together? *(Your last answer times itself)* What would happen if all of those seeds sprouted, too? *(There would be apple trees everywhere.)* Why do plants make so many extra seeds? *(See Background Info, above left.)*

Seeds on the Move

Across

2. Coconuts can _____ for months—long enough to cross an ocean.

4. Along with 14 Across and 15 Down, thing that plants need to survive.

5. _____ helps the columbine scatter its seeds by whipping its seed heads around.

8. The _____ feeds on saguaro fruits and carries their seeds away from the mother plant.

11. When a _____ or boot tracks through the mud, it can give wild-flower seeds a ride.

12. A plant's delicious _____ can attract hungry animals, which can give its seeds a free ride.

13. These hold the beginnings of baby plants inside.

14. Along with 4 Across and 15 Down, things that plants need to survive.

16. A _____ won't sprout until it's out of the ocean, warmed by the sun.

Down

1. Plants growing in the same area have to _____ for what they need to survive.

3. A dandelion seed's fluffy "_____" catches the wind to sail away.

5. This tree can "shoot" its seeds up to 30 feet away.

6. Seeds in _____ can catch a free ride on passing paws or boots.

7. Burdock seedpods are covered with tiny _____ that grab like Velcro.

9. Saguaro seeds drop to the ground with a bat's _____. This will provide fertilizer for the growing plants.

10. A seed has a better chance of growing if it _____ far away from its mother plant.

15. Along with 4 Across and 14 Across, thing that plants need to survive.

They've Got Backbone

Feel the line of bones running up the center of your back. You've just found proof that you're a *vertebrate*, an animal with a backbone. Other vertebrates include elephants, frogs, penguins, and goldfish. Scientists divide vertebrates into five smaller groups based on other typical characteristics. Read the descriptions below.

Amphibians
(more than 4,000 known species)

- have moist, smooth skin.
- lay their eggs in water, where the babies hatch and grow. As they grow, amphibians go through a set of changes called *metamorphosis*. (For instance, a tadpole turns into a frog.) When they become adults, amphibians live mostly on dry land.
- are cold-blooded—their body temperature is affected by their environment. In cold weather, their bodies are cold and sluggish. In hot weather, they may sit in water to cool off.
- get oxygen from the water using gills when they are babies. When they grow into adults, they get oxygen from the air using lungs. All during their lives, they also get some oxygen through their skin.

Birds (more than 9,000 known species)

- have wings that allow them to fly.
- have a streamlined shape, which allows them to slice through the air as they fly.
- have feathers. Along with aiding in flight, feathers help birds keep in body heat.
- have light bones to make flying easier.
- have beaks and scaly legs.
- lay hard-shelled eggs.
- are warm-blooded—their bodies maintain a steady temperature.
- get oxygen from the air using their lungs.

Mammals (about 4,000 known species)

● have hair or fur.
● give birth to live young.
● drink milk made by their mothers' bodies.
● are warm-blooded—their bodies maintain a constant temperature.
● get oxygen from the air using their lungs.

Fish (more than 19,000 known species)

● swim.
● have scales.
● have a streamlined shape, which allows them to slice through water as they swim.
● lay eggs.
● are cold-blooded—their body temperature is affected by their environment.
● get oxygen from the water using gills.

Reptiles (more than 6,000 known species)

● have scales.
● lay leathery eggs. When the babies hatch, they look like tiny adults.
● are cold-blooded—their body temperature is affected by their environment. On a cold day, they're cold and sluggish. They may bask in the sun to warm up. On a hot day, they may sit in the shade to cool off.
● get oxygen from the air using their lungs.

Did You Know?

Animals without backbones—like insects, worms, and jellyfish—are called *invertebrates*. Most animal species in the world are invertebrates. In fact, out of every 100 species on Earth, only about 3 are vertebrates.

Background Info

The characteristics listed on pages 28–29 are *typical* for each group of animals. However, not every species in the group has them all. Scientists classify animals into groups to determine how different species are related. They have constructed a hierarchy of groups, going from largest to smallest: kingdom, phylum, class, order, family, genus, species. There can also be sub-groupings of each. Humans belong to the following groups: kingdom—Animal; phylum—Cordata; subphylum—Vertebrata; order—Primates; suborder—Anthropoidea; family—Hominidae; genus—Homo; species—sapiens.

Amphibians, birds, mammals, and reptiles each make up a class of vertebrates. However, fish are actually divided into three separate classes. The smallest and most primitive class is the *jawless fish (Agnatha)*, like lampreys and hagfish. They have sucker-like mouths, and smooth, slimy skin. Instead of a backbone, fish in this class have a flexible rod of cartilage down their backs. (Cartilage is the same material that shapes your nose and the tops of your outer ears.) Next smallest is *chondrichthyes*, including sharks and ray. These fish have backbones and a skeletal structure, but they are made of cartilage instead of bone. About 95 percent of fish belong to the third class, *osteichthyes* or "bony fish."

Taking It Further

To show the range of variation within these classes of vertebrates, put the names of these mammals on the board: bat, dolphin, duck-billed platypus. Ask: Bats can fly, so why aren't they birds? Dolphins swim, so why aren't they fish? Duck-billed platypuses lay leathery eggs on land, so why aren't they reptiles? Help students see that while these mammals have some very obvious unusual characteristics, they still share a lot in common with other mammals. For instance, bats have hair, not feathers. They give birth to live young. Dolphins are warm-blooded and must rise to the surface to breathe air. Duck-billed platypuses have fur and nurse their young after they hatch.

Crossword Answers

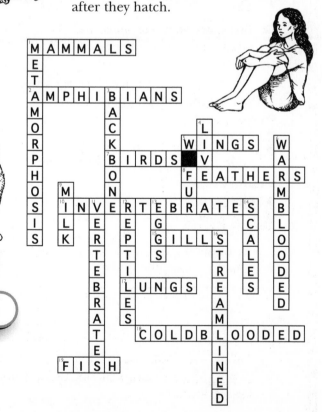

They've Got Backbone

Across

1. Humans belong to this group of vertebrates.

2. Most _____ live in water as babies and on land as adults.

5. Birds have two legs and two _____.

7. Most species of _____ have light bones.

8. These help birds fly and keep them warm.

10. Most animals on Earth don't have backbones. They're called _____.

15. Baby amphibians and fish get oxygen from water using _____.

17. Birds, mammals, reptiles, and adult amphibians use these to get oxygen from the air.

18. _____ animals have a body temperature that is affected by their environment.

19. _____ is the only group of vertebrates where most species spend all of their lives in water.

Down

1. As amphibians grow, they go through a set of changes called _____.

3. This line of bones runs up the middle of your back.

4. Most mammals give birth to _____ young.

6. _____ animals maintain a steady body temperature.

8. Most mammals have _____ or hair.

9. Mammal babies drink _____ from their mothers.

11. Animals with backbones are called _____.

12. When baby _____ hatch, they look like tiny adults.

13. Most amphibians, birds, fish, and reptiles lay _____.

14. Birds have _____ on their legs and feet. Reptiles are covered with them.

16. Birds and fish usually have a _____ shape that helps them slice through air or water.

Sizing Up Whales

How big is a whale? A blue whale is longer than a basketball court. But a beluga whale would fit easily in your classroom. Check out how these and other whales measure up.

◄ BLUE WHALE
TYPE: baleen
FOOD: *krill* (tiny shrimp)
STATUS: endangered
FACT: The blue whale is the largest animal ever known to live. Blue-whale *calves* (babies) gain 200 pounds per day during their first seven months.

MAXIMUM LENGTH: 102 FT

◄ FIN WHALE
TYPE: baleen
FOOD: small fish, krill, *zooplankton* (tiny sea animals)
STATUS: endangered
FACT: These fast swimmers can speed up to 23 miles per hour.

MAXIMUM LENGTH: 80 FT

▲ RIGHT WHALE

TYPE: baleen
FOOD: zooplankton, especially copepods
STATUS: endangered

FACT: Right whales were named by whalers, who thought they were the "right whale" to catch—they were slow swimmers, floated when dead, and had lots of valuable *blubber* (fat).

▲ KILLER WHALE (or ORCA)

TYPE: toothed
FOOD: other whales, seals, fish, birds, squid, and turtles
STATUS: not endangered

FACT: These are the only whales that eat other whales. They can hunt together like wolves, surrounding and attacking large prey, even blue whales.

▲ BELUGA WHALE

TYPE: toothed
FOOD: fish, shellfish, and zooplankton
STATUS: not endangered

FACT: Belugas are known as "sea canaries" because of the many different sounds they make: whistles, squeaks, clucks, mews, chirps, twills, and bell-like tones.

MAXIMUM LENGTH: 50 FT

MAXIMUM LENGTH: 30 FT

MAXIMUM LENGTH: 16 FT

Toothed or Baleen? Here are the main differences between these two groups of whales.

Toothed whales

- get food by hunting or foraging.
- are social animals that often live and hunt in groups called *pods*.
- use *echolocation* to find food. The whales send out sound waves, which bounce off of prey and return to the whale. This helps the whale tell the prey's location.

Baleen whales

- filter food out of the water using baleen plates that look like giant fringe-covered combs. When a baleen whale takes a mouthful of ocean, the water passes out through slits in the baleen, leaving tiny sea creatures behind for the whale to swallow.
- spend most of their time alone or in loose groups.
- don't seem to use echolocation. Since they don't hunt, scientists don't think they need it.

Did You Know?

Whales are not fish. Instead, they're mammals just like you. They breathe air, give birth to live young, and feed their babies milk.

Background Info

Whales are difficult for scientists to study because they spend so much of their lives under the water's surface, where humans can't easily view them. There are about 75 species of whales—about 10 are classified as baleen and the rest are classified as toothed. Scientists think that whales' common mammal ancestor began returning to the water to feed approximately 55 million years ago.

Baleen is made of *keratin*, the same thing as your hair and fingernails.

Taking It Further

Have students tape a piece of paper to the bottom of their graph and add these for comparison:

- diplodocus dinosaur (88 ft)
- triceratops dinosaur (25 ft)
- anaconda (30 ft)
- classic VW Beetle (13 ft)
- basketball court (84 ft)
- your classroom
- students lying down (probably between 4–5 ft)

Whales have a thick layer of *blubber*, or fat, that insulates their bodies in cold ocean water. To show students how well fat insulates, try this class demonstration: Put one cup of room-temperature shortening inside a zip-up sandwich bag. Turn a second bag inside out and place it inside the first, squishing the shortening around until you have an even layer on all sides. "Zip" the bags together to contain the shortening. Take two more sandwich bags and zip them together without any shortening inside. Insert a thermometer into each bag. Then place both bags inside a bowl of icy water, taking care not to allow any of the water into the bag. Have students record the temperature every two minutes. Ask: What happened? *(The temperature inside the insulated bag should drop much more slowly.)* Why do whales, seals, penguins, and polar bears all have thick layers of fat? *(It helps them stay warm.)*

Crossword Answers

Sizing Up Whales

Across

2. Whale fat

5. _____ whales are the largest animals ever known to live.

11. Toothed whales use _____ to find their prey.

12. _____ whales were a favorite target for whalers.

13. Whales aren't fish. They're _____.

14. _____ whales can speed up to 23 miles per hour.

17. The three largest whales on this graph are all _____. That means that they are in danger of dying out.

Down

1. Tiny shrimp

3. Beluga whales are sometimes called _____ because of the sounds they make.

4. _____ whales are social animals, and often live in groups called pods.

6. A group of _____ whales can hunt down and kill much larger blue whales.

7. Fin whales and right whales eat tiny sea animals called _____.

8. _____ whales can grow up to 16 feet.

9. _____ plates look like giant fringe-covered combs.

10. Baleen _____ tiny sea creatures out of the water.

15. Groups of whales

16. Baby whales

On Defense

What would you do if something big and hungry wanted to eat you? Some animals face this problem every day. They're called *prey*, and the animals that hunt them are called *predators*. Read on to learn some tricks prey animals use to stay alive.

Run Fast ▶

For some animals, running away is the best defense. This **basilisk lizard** has an extra advantage. Thanks to flaps of skin on its feet and fast sprinting speeds, it can run across the surface of water to get to safety.

Be a Copycat ▶

Why does this **fly** look so much like a bee? Insect eaters know that bees sting. So if this fly can fool predators into thinking it's a stinging bee, it's home free. This kind of fake-out is called *mimicry*.

Blend In ▲

What a predator can't see, it can't catch and eat. So in the winter, this **snowshoe hare** grows a white fur coat to match the snow. When the snow melts, the hare grows brown fur to match the bare ground. This kind of blending in is called *camouflage*.

Stand Out ▲

Poisonous animals would rather be seen and remembered. This **poison arrow frog's** bright orange markings really stand out against a green leaf. The message? "I'm dangerous. Don't even try to eat me."

◀ Look Big and Bad

This **Io moth** would make a tasty treat for many birds. Those birds, in turn, are tasty to larger predators, like owls. The moth takes advantage of this by flashing the two large eyespots on its wings. If the moth is in luck, the hungry bird will take the spots for glaring owl eyes and fly away.

Suit Up ▲

This **armadillo** is covered with thick, scaly plates that protect it like a suit of armor.

Team Up ▲

Musk oxen are huge and woolly, with large curly horns. But one ox by itself is still no match for a pack of hunting wolves. So the oxen travel in herds of 10 to 20. If wolves attack, the oxen form a circle, with their young safe in the center. Using this teamwork, the oxen can drive off the hungry wolves.

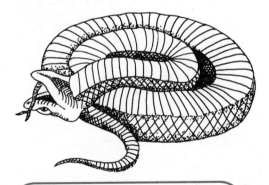

Play Dead ▲

Some predators will only eat animals they catch alive. So when a **hog-nosed snake** is threatened, it rolls over and pretends to be dead. Once the predator leaves, the snake flips back over and slithers safely away.

Fight Back ▲

The **African porcupine's** back is covered with sharp spines. If a predator threatens, the porcupine can charge backward and give its attacker a nose full of needles.

Background Info

Sometimes several species will "pool" their defensive resources. For instance, on the open savannas of Africa, ostriches, kudus, and zebras can often be seen grazing and browsing together. Each species wants to stay safe from predators such as lions, spotted hyenas, and cape hunting dogs. When they can all rely on the ostrich's excellent eyesight, the kudu's keen hearing, and the zebra's great sense of smell, they stand a much better chance of survival.

There are two main kinds of insect mimicry: Batesian and Mullerian. Batesian mimics are like the fly on page 36. These harmless insects have an advantage because they look like dangerous or distasteful insects. (Some Batesian mimics even look like inanimate objects. For instance, the treehopper looks like a thorn.) Mullerian mimics, in contrast, are also distasteful themselves. Still, it's beneficial for them to mimic other distasteful insects. That's because a predator will sometimes need to eat a distasteful insect to learn its lesson. When that happens, one insect is sacrificed, but any others that look like it—even those of a different species—are one predator safer.

Taking It Further

As a class, brainstorm ways that animal defenses are similar to human defenses. Some ideas:
- snowshoe hare—army camouflage
- poison arrow frog—bright orange hunting jackets
- bee-mimicking fly—soldiers have been known to dress up in another army's uniforms to sneak behind enemy lines
- Io moth—some modern "scarecrows" have exaggerated eyespots
- African porcupine—spears and arrows
- basilisk lizard—any technological advance that helps us move faster
- hog-nosed snake—injured soldiers have been known to "play dead" until an enemy moves on
- armadillo—armor, helmets, bullet-proof vests, tanks, etc.

Crossword Answers

On Defense

Across

1. The _____ is protected by a scaly suit of armor.

3. Animals that are hunted by other animals

7. The _____ drives away predators by playing dead.

10. Insect eaters know that _____ sting. So they might not try to catch a fly that looks like one.

11. _____ travel in herds for safety. If wolves attack, they form a circle with their young in the middle.

13. In the winter, a snowshoe hare has _____ fur.

14. An animal that hunts other animals

Down

2. When one animal protects itself by looking like a more dangerous animal, that's called _____.

4. For some animals, like basilisk lizards, _____ away is the best defense.

5. Many _____ animals are brightly colored so that predators see and remember them.

6. When an animal has a color or pattern that blends in with its environment, that's called _____.

8. The Io moth scares away birds by flashing its large _____.

9. An African porcupine defends itself using sharp _____ that cover its back.

12. If an Io moth is lucky, a hungry bird will be tricked into thinking that it's being attacked by an _____.

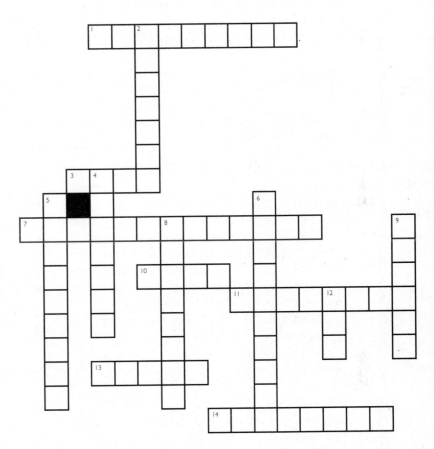

Rain Forest Layers

What's life like in a rain forest? It depends how far off the ground you live. Read on to learn more.

Harpy Eagle
builds its nest atop a rain forest's tallest trees. From there, the harpy eagle can swoop down into the canopy and catch monkeys and other animals.

◀ Red-eyed Tree Frog
hops from tree to tree with the help of its long, strong legs. It visits bromeliads and large leaves, looking for tasty insects and water.

◀ Jaguar
is at the top of a rain forest's food chain. Nothing hunts it, except people. Jaguars prowl the understory for sloths, monkeys, and rats. They also hunt along river-banks for fish, turtles, and caimans.

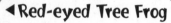

Leaf-cutter Ants
cut off chunks of leaves and drag them into their underground colonies. There, they chew up the leaves and spit them into a kind of fungus "garden." The fungi eat the leaves, and the ants later eat the fungi.

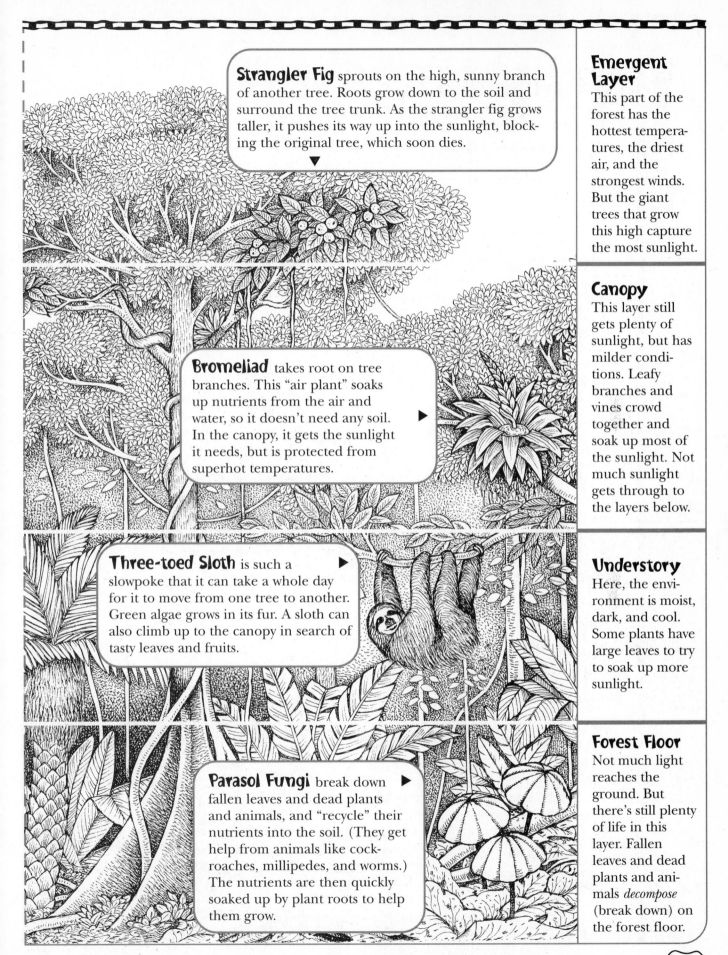

Strangler Fig sprouts on the high, sunny branch of another tree. Roots grow down to the soil and surround the tree trunk. As the strangler fig grows taller, it pushes its way up into the sunlight, blocking the original tree, which soon dies.

▼

Bromeliad takes root on tree branches. This "air plant" soaks up nutrients from the air and water, so it doesn't need any soil. In the canopy, it gets the sunlight it needs, but is protected from superhot temperatures. ▶

Three-toed Sloth is such a ▶ slowpoke that it can take a whole day for it to move from one tree to another. Green algae grows in its fur. A sloth can also climb up to the canopy in search of tasty leaves and fruits.

Parasol Fungi break down ▶ fallen leaves and dead plants and animals, and "recycle" their nutrients into the soil. (They get help from animals like cockroaches, millipedes, and worms.) The nutrients are then quickly soaked up by plant roots to help them grow.

Emergent Layer

This part of the forest has the hottest temperatures, the driest air, and the strongest winds. But the giant trees that grow this high capture the most sunlight.

Canopy

This layer still gets plenty of sunlight, but has milder conditions. Leafy branches and vines crowd together and soak up most of the sunlight. Not much sunlight gets through to the layers below.

Understory

Here, the environment is moist, dark, and cool. Some plants have large leaves to try to soak up more sunlight.

Forest Floor

Not much light reaches the ground. But there's still plenty of life in this layer. Fallen leaves and dead plants and animals *decompose* (break down) on the forest floor.

Background Info

By definition, rain forests receive more than 80 inches of precipitation per year. That sounds like a lot, but 150 inches per year is common. There are rain forests in North and South America, Asia, Australia, New Zealand, and Africa. Tropical rain forests (like the one on pages 40–41) grow near the equator. There are also temperate rain forests (including some in coastal Alaska) that are cold part of the year.

Rain forests are amazingly diverse. They cover less than 6 percent of Earth, but are home to more than half of our known species. Many of those species can't live anywhere else.

Taking It Further

Make a bulletin board of the four layers of a rain forest. Have students research these other rain-forest animals and place their own drawings of them in the correct layer: tapir (forest floor), poison arrow frog (canopy, understory, or forest floor), large wolf spider (understory or forest floor), black caiman (forest floor), margay (canopy or understory), keel-billed toucan (canopy), howler monkey (emergent layer or canopy), emerald tree boa (understory or canopy), quetzal (emergent layer).

Many groups of indigenous people live in the rain forest. Have students research one—like the Yanomani of the Amazon or the Penan of Borneo, Southeast Asia—to see how humans have adapted to this habitat.

Crossword Answers

Crossword grid answers:
- SUNLIGHT
- HARPY
- PARASOLFUNGI
- BROMELIAD
- GARDEN
- JAGUAR
- REDEYEDTREEFROG
- FORESTFLOOR
- UNDERSTORY
- THREETOEDSLOTH
- EMERGENTLAYER
- CANOPY
- NUTRIENTS
- RECYCLE
- STRANGLERFIG

Rain Forest Layers

Across

3. _____ help break down fallen leaves and dead plants and animals.

4. A _____ gets its nutrients from air and water.

5. Leaf-cutter ants grow fungus in a kind of "_____."

6. The _____ hunts in the understory and on the forest floor.

9. The _____ drinks water trapped by large leaves and bromeliads.

10. Leaves, dead plants, and dead animals fall to this layer.

12. In this dark, moist rain-forest layer, some plants have huge leaves to soak up more sunlight.

14. The _____ hangs upside-down along branches in the understory.

16. In the _____, you'll find the most sunlight, hottest temperatures, driest air, and strongest winds.

17. The leaves in this layer capture most of the sunlight.

18. The _____ kills the tree it grows on.

Down

1. Little _____ reaches the understory or the forest floor.

2. The _____ swoops down into the canopy to catch its food.

7. _____ grows in the fur of the three-toed sloth.

8. The _____ takes chunks of leaves into its underground colonies, but doesn't eat them.

11. Most plants get these from the soil. But air plants get them from air or water.

13. Fungi "_____" nutrients into the soil.

15. No other animal besides humans _____ jaguars.

Desert Survival

Plants and animals need water to survive. So how can anything live in a desert, which has hardly any water? Check out these amazing desert plants and animals, and the surprising adaptations that help them stay alive.

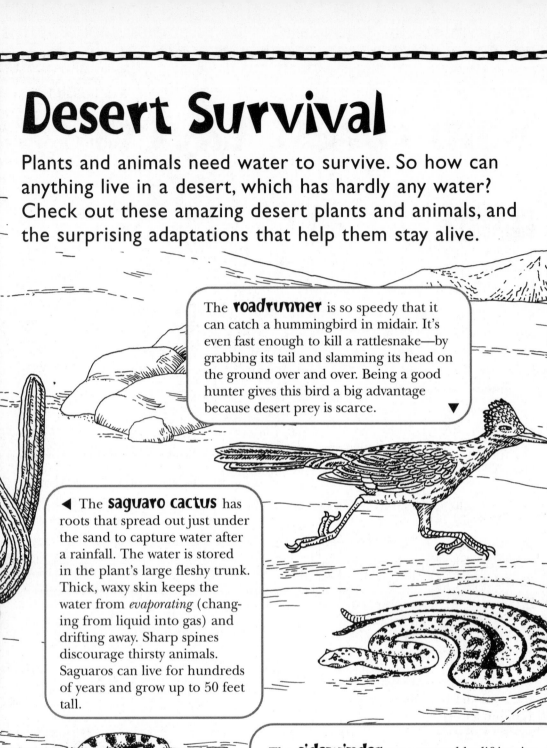

The **roadrunner** is so speedy that it can catch a hummingbird in midair. It's even fast enough to kill a rattlesnake—by grabbing its tail and slamming its head on the ground over and over. Being a good hunter gives this bird a big advantage because desert prey is scarce. ▼

◄ The **saguaro cactus** has roots that spread out just under the sand to capture water after a rainfall. The water is stored in the plant's large fleshy trunk. Thick, waxy skin keeps the water from *evaporating* (changing from liquid into gas) and drifting away. Sharp spines discourage thirsty animals. Saguaros can live for hundreds of years and grow up to 50 feet tall.

The **sidewinder** gets around by lifting its ▲ body off the sand and moving sideways. This keeps it from slipping in the shifting sand. Very little of the snake's body touches the hot sand at any time. This helps keep it cool. The sidewinder gets its water from juicy prey, such as lizards, mice, and kangaroo rats. It's *nocturnal*, or active at night. During the day, it slips into a burrow dug by another animal or rests under a shady bush.

The **ocotillo** sits dormant during dry spells. As soon as enough rain comes, it quickly grows leaves to make food. The plant uses the food to grow flowers, quickly followed by seeds. The ocotillo then drops its leaves and becomes dormant again until the next rain. ◀

The **creosote bush** is an expert at removing water from the desert sand. The sand around this bush becomes so dry that often no other plants can survive in it. ▼

▲ A **jackrabbit's** long ears are filled with blood vessels. When the rabbit rests in the shade, heat leaves the warm blood in the vessels and is carried away by the cooler air.

The **desert pupfish** lives in ▶ rare desert streams and pools. The shallow water in the streams is hot, but pupfish can survive water temperatures of up to 112°F. When the water gets chilly in winter, pupfish must burrow into the mud and become *dormant* (go into a deep sleep).

◀ The **kangaroo rat** never drinks water. It gets whatever water it needs from its food, such as the saguaro fruit, or even seeds. Long passageways inside the kangaroo rat's nose capture moisture from the air. That keeps the animal from losing water when it breathes out. The kangaroo rat is nocturnal. It spends its days resting in an underground burrow, where the air is cool and moist.

Background Info

Deserts are the second-most diverse ecosystem, after rain forests. Because of the scarcity of water, deserts are tough places to live. But plants and animals have developed some amazing adaptations to help them acquire and retain water. A plant's main danger from high desert temperatures is increased evaporation. But animals have to battle high body temperatures as well. Many can survive higher body temperatures than their relatives in cooler climates. Desert animals have also developed many ways of both avoiding heat and cooling off.

Crossword Answers

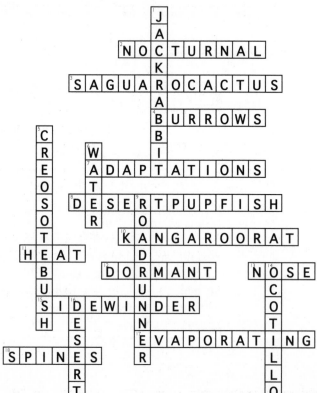

Taking It Further

As a class, review the adaptations listed on page 44–45. Which are *behavioral* adaptations—special ways that the animal acts that allow it to survive in the desert? Which are *physiological* adaptations—special body features that make it more fit for desert life?

Saguaro cactus trunks are pleated like an accordion. This allows the trunk to swell during wet times and shrink during dry times. To demonstrate how this works, cut a 10-by-1-in. strip of paper. Pleat it like an accordion. (Make each pleat about 1/2 in. wide.) Tape the ends together to make a circle. This is like a cross section of a saguaro's trunk. Place it on a table and have one student volunteer hold the sides steady while another pours beans into it. Ask: As more beans fill the paper saguaro, what happens to the trunk? *(The pleats unfold and the size of the trunk expands.)* How is this like what happens to a real saguaro after a rainfall? *(The extra water makes the trunk swell the same way.)* What might happen to the saguaro if its skin weren't pleated? *(It wouldn't be able to hold the extra water. If it tried, the skin would burst.)*

Desert Survival

Across

2. _____ animals are active at night.

3. A _____ stores water in its large, fleshy trunk.

4. Both kangaroo rats and sidewinders keep out of the hot sun by hiding in _____.

7. Desert plants and animals have special _____ to help then survive in their environment.

8. The _____ can survive water temperatures of up to 112°F.

10. The _____ gets water from food, such as saguaro fruits and seeds.

11. A jackrabbit uses its long ears to get rid of this.

12. Both the ocotillo and desert pupfish cope with desert life by becoming _____ at times.

13. Long passageways inside a kangaroo rat's _____ keep it from losing water when it breathes.

15. The _____ has a special way of traveling through a desert's shifting sands.

17. A saguaro's thick, waxy skin keeps the water inside its trunk from _____.

18. Sharp _____ discourage animals from eating pieces of juicy saguaro cactus.

Down

1. A _____ has longer ears that help it cool off.

5. The _____ leaves the sand around itself so dry that often nothing else can live nearby.

6. All plants and animals need _____.

9. A _____ is such a fast hunter that it can catch a flying hummingbird or kill a rattlesnake.

14. This plant only grows leaves right after sufficient rainfall.

16. Plants and animals who live in a _____ have to deal with scarce water and superhot temperatures.

Under the Sea

Dive into these four ocean layers to see what can survive in each.

Phytoplankton are microscopic plants that make food using energy from sunlight. Phytoplankton form the base of the ocean food chain. ▶

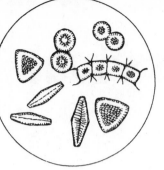

▼ A **great white shark** swims deep in the sunlit zone. Its dark-gray back blends in with the dark water around it, making it invisible from above. When the shark spots the outline of prey passing overhead, it launches a surprise attack from below.

▲ **Zooplankton** are tiny animals that feed on phytoplankton. Some zooplankton are newly hatched babies that grow into larger fish and shrimp.

Anchovies skim just below the ocean's surface, scooping up phytoplankton and zooplankton. They, in turn, are bite-sized snacks for larger fish, like mackerel. ▶

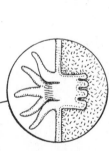

▲ **Coral polyps** are tiny animals that live together in colonies. When they die, they leave behind a hard skeleton. A new layer of coral polyps grow on top of these shells. Over the years, the polyps build large coral reefs, which are home to many sea creatures.

Sunlit Zone

This warm and sunny zone supports most of the life in the ocean.

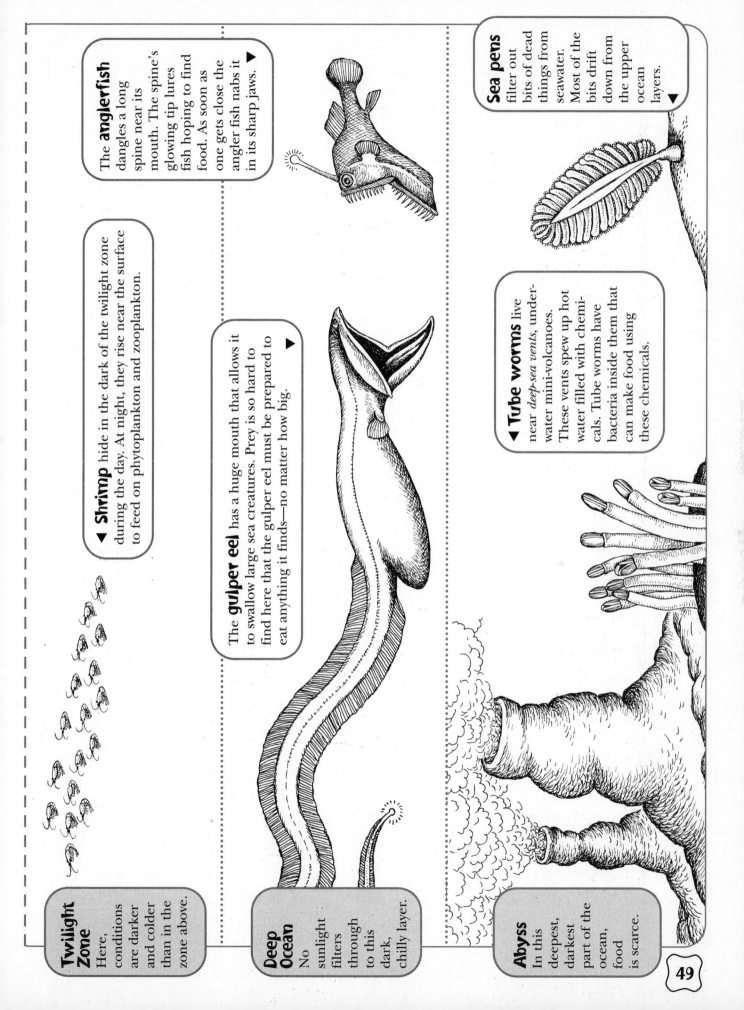

The anglerfish dangles a long spine near its mouth. The spine's glowing tip lures fish hoping to find food. As soon as one gets close the angler fish nabs it in its sharp jaws. ▶

Sea pens filter out bits of dead things from seawater. Most of the bits drift down from the upper ocean layers. ▼

▶ **Shrimp** hide in the dark of the twilight zone during the day. At night, they rise near the surface to feed on phytoplankton and zooplankton.

The **gulper eel** has a huge mouth that allows it to swallow large sea creatures. Prey is so hard to find here that the gulper eel must be prepared to eat anything it finds—no matter how big. ▶

▶ **Tube worms** live near *deep-sea vents*, underwater mini-volcanoes. These vents spew up hot water filled with chemicals. Tube worms have bacteria inside them that can make food using these chemicals.

Twilight Zone
Here, conditions are darker and colder than in the zone above.

Deep Ocean
No sunlight filters through to this dark, chilly layer.

Abyss
In this deepest, darkest part of the ocean, food is scarce.

Background Info

About 70 percent of the Earth is covered with sea water. However, the ocean is the hardest environment on Earth for scientists to study because of its vastness and severe conditions.

One of the biggest obstacles to ocean exploration is *water pressure*. As divers descend, the water above presses on them. The lower they go—and the more water above them—the higher the water pressure. Because of this, most scuba divers don't swim below 130 feet—not even halfway down into the sunlit zone. To study deeper regions, scientists invented sturdy subs that can survive superhigh water pressure.

Water pressure adds an extra challenge to studying creatures adapted for the deepest depths. Because they are used to such high pressure, these animals often can't survive a trip to the surface, so scientists can't bring up live samples to observe.

The depth of the ocean varies from region to region, the areas near the shore being more shallow. The average ocean depth is just over 12,000 ft.

Taking It Further

Challenge students to make a graph that compares the relative sizes of the four ocean zones:

- sunlit zone goes from 0–500 ft down
- twilight zone goes from 500–3,000 ft down
- deep ocean goes from 3,000–13,000 ft down
- abyss goes from 13,000–38,000 ft down.

They may choose to make a bar graph with four bars, or stack the bars on top of one another, making a cross section.

Crossword Answers

Under the Sea

Across

1. The deepest, darkest ocean zone

3. _____ filter out scraps drifting down through the ocean water.

4. The _____ can swallow prey larger than itself.

5. Some light gets through to this ocean zone, but not much.

8. Like the anglerfish, many animals in this totally dark zone have body parts that glow.

12. The _____ swims through the lower part of the sunlit zone, looking for prey above.

15. Tiny sea animals that eat phytoplankton

Down

2. The ocean zone that supports the most life

3. This animal may hide in the twilight zone during the day.

6. _____ skim just under the ocean's surface, swallowing phytoplankton and zooplankton.

7. The _____ "fishes" for prey using a spine with a glowing tip.

9. Over the years, tiny _____ build large coral reefs.

10. _____ spew hot water filled with chemicals.

11. Most sea creatures depend on these tiny plants for survival.

13. _____ are filled with bacteria that make food using chemicals from deep-sea vents.

14. Phytoplankton make food using energy from _____.

Volcano

What can make a sleepy-looking mountain erupt into a hotheaded volcano? Follow the numbered steps to find out. (Hint: Start at the bottom.)

7. Any eruption can change the shape of a volcano. Many large ones hollow out large craters called **calderas**. Sometimes, these craters fill with water and become peaceful-looking lakes. But underneath, the volcano may be building toward another blast.

6. Large volcanic eruptions are sometimes surrounded by **lightning**. That's because the flying ash and rocks rub together, producing *static electricity*. When enough static electricity builds up . . . *FLASH!* Lightning discharges it.

5. When magma reaches the surface, the gases explode out of it. With this blast of gas can come chunks of rock, globs of hot magma (now called **lava**), and **volcanic ash** (tiny pieces of lava). As the lava falls, it may cool into teardrop-shaped rocks called **volcanic bombs**. Some are as small as peas, some larger than minivans.

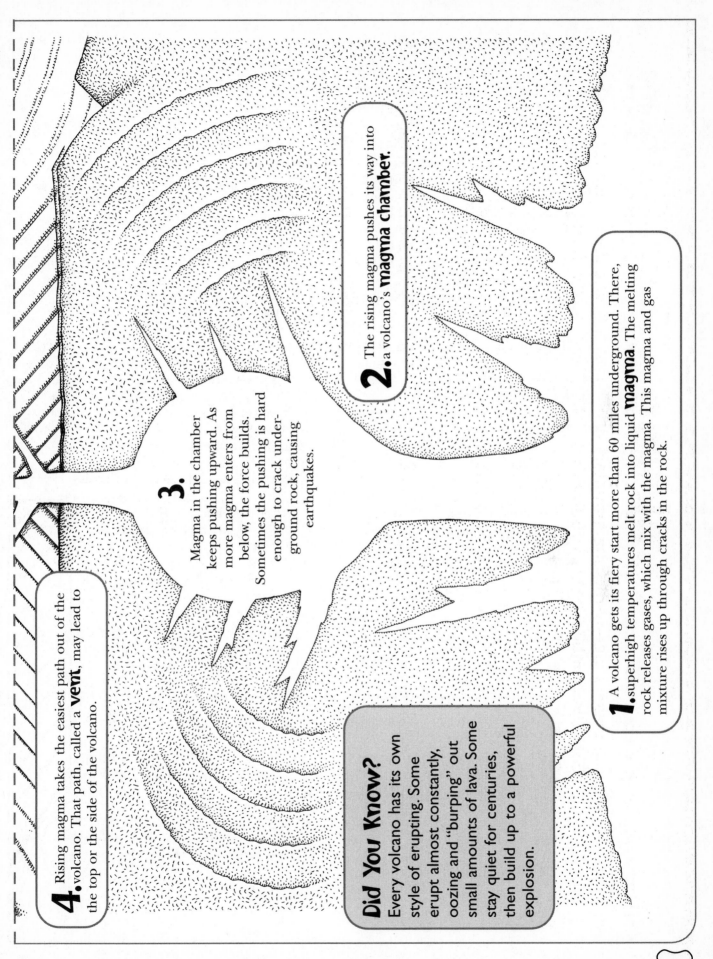

2. The rising magma pushes its way into a volcano's **magma chamber.**

3. Magma in the chamber keeps pushing upward. As more magma enters from below, the force builds. Sometimes the pushing is hard enough to crack underground rock, causing earthquakes.

1. A volcano gets its fiery start more than 60 miles underground. There, superhigh temperatures melt rock into liquid **magma.** The melting rock releases gases, which mix with the magma. This magma and gas mixture rises up through cracks in the rock.

4. Rising magma takes the easiest path out of the volcano. That path, called a **vent,** may lead to the top or the side of the volcano.

Did You Know?
Every volcano has its own style of erupting. Some erupt almost constantly, oozing and "burping" out small amounts of lava. Some stay quiet for centuries, then build up to a powerful explosion.

Background Info

Magma rises largely because it is less dense (lighter for the same volume) than the rock around it. There are two reasons for this difference in density. First, when rock melts it expands, so a cup of melted rock would weigh less than a cup of solid rock. Second, the hot gases mixed in with the magma make it even less dense.

Volcanic ash has no relationship to ash from burning wood. It received that name because it superficially resembles wood ash. If you looked at volcanic ash under a microscope, you would see that it is made of tiny shards of *obsidian*, a type of glass that is created when lava cools rapidly.

Here are some interesting volcano facts to share with your class:

● There are 10 times as many volcanoes under the ocean than there are on land.
● Each year, about 50 volcanoes erupt.
● Some volcanoes blow with more energy than hundreds of atomic bombs.
● Molten lava can flow as fast as 35 miles per hour.

Taking It Further

Have students hold their breath for as long as they can. At some point, the air in their lungs will "erupt" out of their mouths. Ask: How is this like an explosive volcano? *(Pressure builds up and is released all at once.)* Students may notice that some classmates can hold their breath longer than others. Explain that it's natural for different people to have different lung capacities, and that some medical conditions (such as asthma) can affect how long an individual can hold his or her breath.

To show students how air can explode out of a liquid, take them outside and shake a can of club soda or other carbonated water. Point the can away from the class and open it. Ask: How do you know gas was released from the liquid? *(Hissing sound, bubbles)* What came out with the gas? *(Some of the liquid)* Back in the classroom, pass around a piece of pumice stone. (Pumice is available in many drug and beauty stores for sloughing off dead skin.) Explain that it came from a volcano. Ask: What evidence do you see that there was gas mixed with this rock? *(Holes)*

Crossword Answers

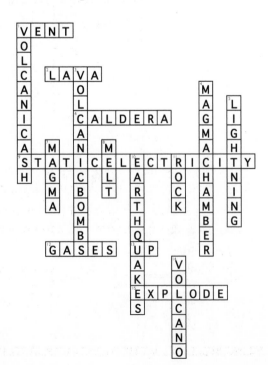

Volcano

Across

1. The path that magma travels along is called a _____.

2. Magma is called _____ after it reaches the surface.

6. Large eruptions often leave behind a _____.

9. Lightning strikes when a lot of built-up _____ is discharged.

12. When rock melts into magma, it releases _____.

13. The direction magma travels

15. When magma reaches the surface, gases _____ out of it.

Down

1. Tiny pieces of lava

3. Large, falling chunks of lava

4. Melted rock collects in a volcano's _____.

5. Because of churning rock and ash, the largest volcanic eruptions are sometimes surrounded by _____.

7. Melted rock inside a volcano

8. Superhigh temperatures _____ underground rock into liquid magma.

10. Pressure from rising magma can crack underground rock, causing _____.

11. A volcanic eruption can have a mixture of gases, lava, volcanic ash, and chunks of _____.

14. Each _____ has its own style of erupting.

The Solar System

Meet Earth's neighboring planets

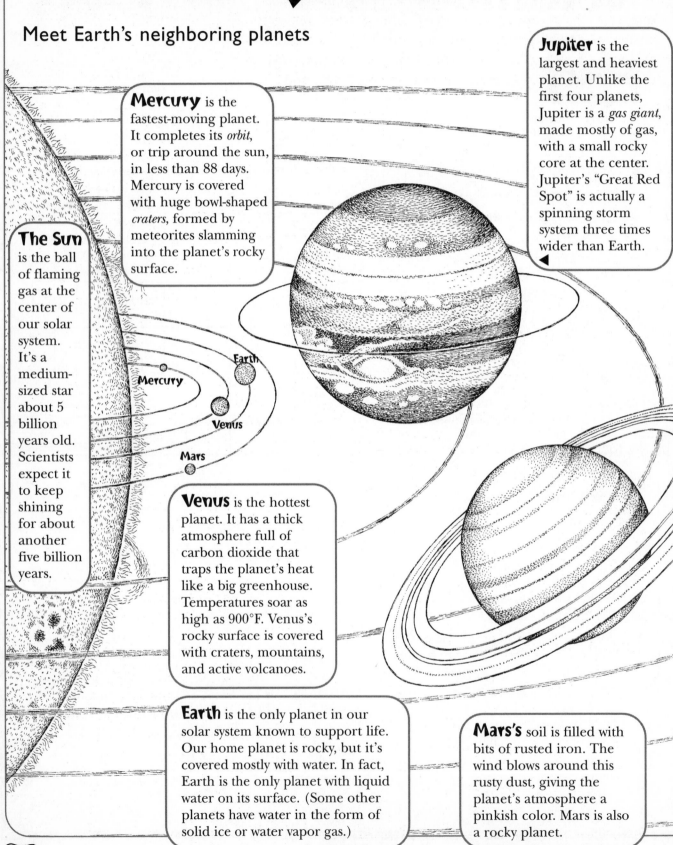

Jupiter is the largest and heaviest planet. Unlike the first four planets, Jupiter is a *gas giant*, made mostly of gas, with a small rocky core at the center. Jupiter's "Great Red Spot" is actually a spinning storm system three times wider than Earth.

Mercury is the fastest-moving planet. It completes its *orbit*, or trip around the sun, in less than 88 days. Mercury is covered with huge bowl-shaped *craters*, formed by meteorites slamming into the planet's rocky surface.

The Sun is the ball of flaming gas at the center of our solar system. It's a medium-sized star about 5 billion years old. Scientists expect it to keep shining for about another five billion years.

Venus is the hottest planet. It has a thick atmosphere full of carbon dioxide that traps the planet's heat like a big greenhouse. Temperatures soar as high as 900°F. Venus's rocky surface is covered with craters, mountains, and active volcanoes.

Earth is the only planet in our solar system known to support life. Our home planet is rocky, but it's covered mostly with water. In fact, Earth is the only planet with liquid water on its surface. (Some other planets have water in the form of solid ice or water vapor gas.)

Mars's soil is filled with bits of rusted iron. The wind blows around this rusty dust, giving the planet's atmosphere a pinkish color. Mars is also a rocky planet.

Did You Know?

Any time you see all of the planets in one diagram, such as this one, something important is wrong. The distances between the planets are much smaller than they should be. An artist would say the drawing is "not to scale." If this diagram were to scale, the solar system would stretch out over nearly a mile and a half.

Pluto has long been considered the odd-ball of the solar system. It's the smallest planet by far. Its orbit is unusually elliptical and tilted. Plus, it's the only planet made largely of ice. Now, scientists say that Pluto isn't really a planet at all. Instead, it's a very big piece of leftover comet, called a *Kuiper* (COY-per) *Belt object.*
▼

◄ **Uranus** is tilted on its side, so that sometimes its north pole points almost directly at the sun. This gas giant is made partly of a gas called *methane*, which gives it a blue-green color.

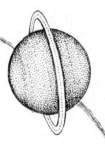

◄ **Saturn** is a gas giant famous for its spectacular rings. The rings are made of icy lumps, some pebble-sized and others as big as a school bus. The rings are only about a mile wide, but they reach out about 260,000 miles from the planet's surface.

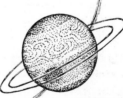

▲ **Neptune** is the last gas giant. It's usually the eighth planet, as shown here. However, Pluto's extra-*elliptical* (oval-shaped) orbit sometimes brings it closer to the sun than Neptune. So for 20 out of every 248 years, Neptune becomes the farthest planet from the sun.

Background Info

The planets in our solar system orbit the sun. Most of the planets, in turn, are orbited by moons. (Saturn has the most, with 18 confirmed satellites.) Scientists have found mathematical evidence of planets around nearby stars, but can't hope to study them in any detail with today's technology.

Scientists have discovered about 75 other Kuiper Belt objects, all much smaller than Pluto, just outside of Neptune's orbit.

Here are some other things that are "wrong" with most solar system diagrams: The planets are very, very seldom lined up on the same side of the sun. In addition, some diagrams don't show the planets to scale in relation to one another. (Ours does. The scale we used was 1 cm = 25,000 km.)

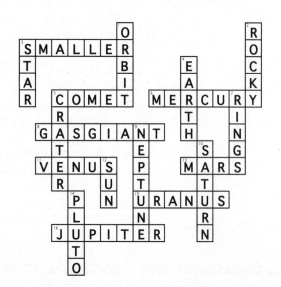

Crossword Answers

Taking It Further

To give students a better idea of the vast distances in the solar system, try making a scale model of the solar system. Hold up a copy of the diagram and explain that the planets are not to scale. Have students predict how large an area your class would need to make a scale model. Would the model fit in their classroom? Would they need to use the whole school building? The whole school-yard? Cut out a circle 56 cm in diameter. This will be your sun. Then cut out each planet from the diagram. Have students guess how far away the first planet, Mercury, should go. After predictions are in, share this figure: In our scale model, Mercury should be 23.16 meters (about 35 average 10-year-old walking steps) away from the sun. Do students want to make new predictions about how large their scale model will be? Depending on the size of your schoolyard, you can plot out some more of the solar system using these figures:

- Venus—43.2 m (65 steps) from the sun
- Earth—60 m (90 steps)
- Mars—91.6 m (137 steps)
- Jupiter—311.6 m (467 steps)
- Saturn—571.6 m (857 steps)
- Uranus—1,150 m (1,725 steps)
- Neptune—1,798.4 m (2,698 steps)
- Pluto—2,365.2 m (3,548 steps)

Altogether, you'd need nearly 1 1/2 miles to make this model to scale!

The Solar System

Across

3. This drawing is not to scale. It shows the distances between the planets _____ than they actually are.

5. Scientists now say that Pluto is really a piece of leftover _____, not a planet.

6. The fastest-moving planet

8. Jupiter is a _____. So are Saturn, Uranus, and Neptune.

11. This planet has a lot of carbon dioxide in its atmosphere. This gas traps the planet's heat, making it the hottest planet in the solar system.

13. Rusty dust gives this planet's atmosphere a pinkish color.

15. This planet is tilted.

16. The largest and heaviest planet

Down

1. A planet's trip around the sun is called its _____.

2. Mercury, Venus, Earth, and Mars are all _____ planets.

3. The sun is a _____.

4. The only planet that we know can support life

5. When a meteorite slams into a rocky planet's surface, it makes a _____.

7. Saturn's _____ are made of icy lumps.

9. This planet is usually the eighth planet, but sometimes it's the ninth instead.

10. This planet is famous for its rings.

12. The planets in our solar system all orbit the _____.

14. This small, oddball planet is made mostly of ice.

What's the Weather?

Rain? Snow? Sun? A weather map can tell you what to expect—if you know how to read it.

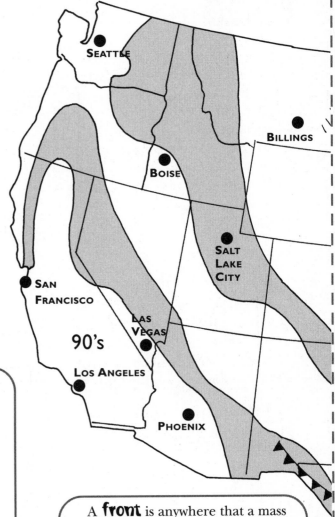

The light and dark areas are **temperature bands.** Everywhere within each band has a temperature in the same range. The number tells what the range is. For instance, every place in the 80's temperature band has thermometer readings of 80 to 89 degrees Fahrenheit.

KEY:

 rain

 snow

 cold front

 warm front

A **key** tells you what each symbol on a map means. Find the symbols in the key for the two most common kinds of precipitation—rain and snow. Can you find an example of each on the map?

A **front** is anywhere that a mass of cold air meets a mass of warm air. At a **stationary front,** the two masses aren't moving very much.

Did You Know?

A cup of warm air actually weighs less than a cup of cold air. Scientists say the warm air is *less dense* than cold air. Because warm air is *less dense*, it can actually float on cold air. That's why hot-air balloons rise. It's also why a cold front can push warm air upwards.

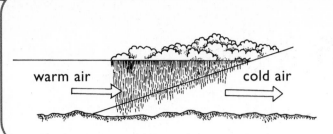

At a **warm front**, warm air is replacing cold air. As the warm air pushes forward, some of it rises over the retreating cold air. As with a cold front, the rising warm air forms clouds. But these clouds are more widely spread out. So warm fronts often bring steady rain to a large area. After a warm front passes, the weather usually turns warmer.

▼

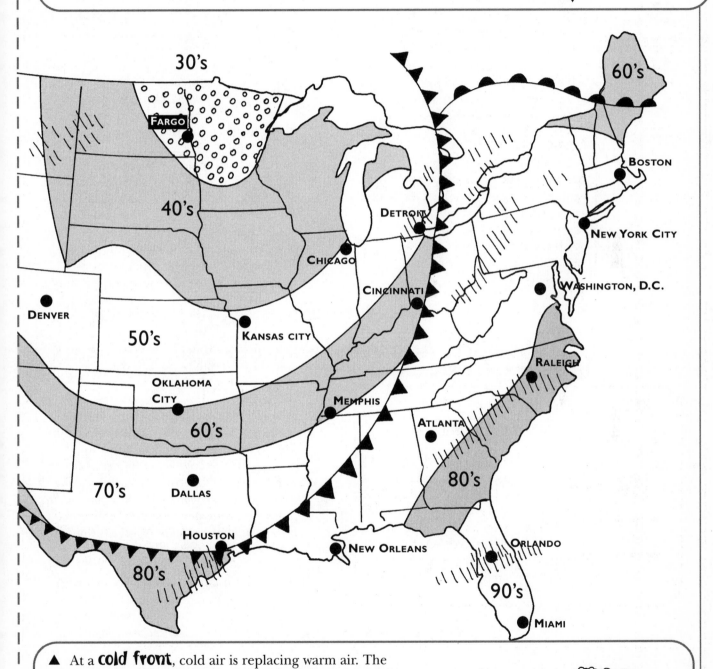

▲ At a **cold front**, cold air is replacing warm air. The cold air plows under the warm air, pushing it up and out of the way. Water vapor gas in the quickly rising warm air *condenses* (turns to tiny drops of liquid water), forming huge clouds directly over the front. Cold fronts often bring hard rain and thunderstorms. After a cold front passes, the weather usually turns cooler and drier.

Background Info

Weather systems tend to move across the continental U.S. from west to east. That's because most of the U.S. is in the northern hemisphere's middle latitudes, which have prevailing westerly winds. (Florida is between the middle and lower latitudes. It sometimes has prevailing easterly winds, especially in the summer.)

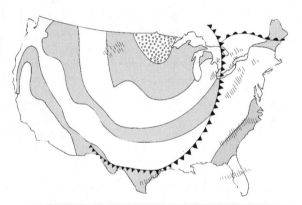

Crossword Answers

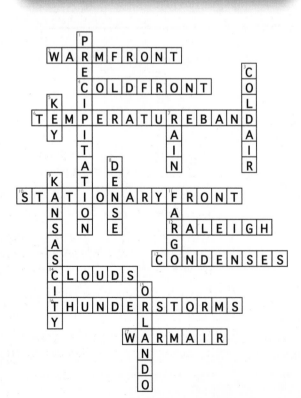

Taking It Further

As with warm air and cold air, warm water is less dense than cold water. Kids can explore this phenomenon with this experiment: Give each group a cup half-filled with warm tap water, a cup half-filled with cold ice water, and a third cup of water for rinsing. Add five drops of red food coloring to the warm water and five drops of blue food coloring to the cold water. Give each student a clear straw. Have students practice "picking up" the clear water by dipping one end of their straw about 1/2 in. in the water, capping the other end with a thumb, and lifting. When they get the hang of it, have students "pick up" 1/2 in. of warm water, then dip the straw about 1 in. into the cold water to pick up some cold water. After they cap the end and lift, what do they see? *(A layer of warm red water over a layer of cold blue water.)* They can release that water into the cup of clear water, and then repeat the experiment, this time picking up the cold water before the warm. What happens? *(As the warm water rises and the cold water sinks, they may mix to purple. Students may even see a band of red water that has risen to the top and a band of blue water that has sunk to the bottom.)*

Have students collect a week's worth of national weather maps from a newspaper. Can they track a front as it moves? What else do they notice?

What's the Weather?

Across

2. After a _____ passes, the weather usually gets warmer.

4. After a _____ passes, the weather usually turns cooler and drier.

6. Salt Lake City, Oklahoma City, Memphis, and Cincinnati are all in the same _____.

10. At a _____, a cold air mass and a warm air mass meet but don't move.

12. In which city would a T-shirt and shorts be most comfortable: Chicago, Minneapolis, or Raleigh?

13. When water vapor _____, it turns into tiny drops of liquid water.

14. When the water vapor in rising air condenses, it forms _____.

16. Cold fronts often bring hard rain and _____.

17. _____ rises over cold air.

Down

1. Rain and snow are both types of _____.

3. At a cold front, _____ pushes warm air up and out of the way.

5. A _____ tells you about the symbols on a map.

7. A warm front often brings steady _____ over a large area.

8. Warm air is less _____ than cold air. That allows warm air to float on cold air.

9. According to the weather map, these cities have temperatures in the 50's: Billings, Denver, _____, and Detroit.

11. According to the weather map, it's snowing in this city.

15. According to the weather map, it's raining in these three cities: Raleigh, Detroit, and _____.

Notes